A WINNING SKILLS BOOK

You Can Be Smart!

Joy Berry

Illustrated by Bartholomew

Joy Berry Enterprises

Copyright © Joy Berry, 2022
Originally Published 2013

All rights are reserved.

No part of this book can be duplicated or used without the prior written permission of the copyright owner, except for the use of brief quotations from the book.

For inquiries or permission requests contact the publisher.

Published by Joy Berry Enterprises
www.joyberryenterprises.com

Joy Berry
Enterprises

INTRODUCTION 3

You can be smart if you understand
- what makes a person smart,
- ten guidelines for becoming a smart person,
- sources of new information, and
- four ways to consider the source.

WHAT MAKES A PERSON SMART

Some people think that a smart person is someone who knows a lot of information.

In reality, some smart people know a lot of information. However, it is *not* this quality that makes them smart.

Some people think that a smart person is someone who has a high IQ (intelligence quotient).

In reality, some smart people have high IQs, but it is *not* this quality that makes them smart.

WHAT MAKES A PERSON SMART

Some people think that a smart person is one who performs well in academic situations such as school.

In reality, some smart people perform well in academic situations. However it is *not* this quality that makes them smart.

Many of the smartest people in the world do not know a lot of information.

Many of the smartest people in the world do not perform well in academic situations.

WHAT MAKES A PERSON SMART

A smart person is one who has the ability and self-discipline to learn **relevant information.** Relevant information is information that helps a person
- survive and grow,
- accomplish necessary tasks and worthwhile goals,
- develop and maintain healthy relationships with others, and
- enjoy life.

A smart person is one who has the ability and self-discipline to put to *use* the relevant information he or she has learned.

Anyone, including you, can be a truly smart person by following several simple guidelines.

Guideline #1: Smart people determine which information is relevant and thus important for them to know. They focus their attention on learning relevant information and do not waste time learning information that is not relevant to them.

Guideline#2: Smart people realize that no one person can know everything there is to know. As a result, when they do not know something, they admit it and are not embarrassed.

Guideline #3: Smart people realize that others might know information they do not know. Therefore, they ask questions when they do not know something.

Guideline #4: Smart people listen carefully to the answers to their questions. To them it is more important to learn than to impress others with what they already know.

TEN GUIDELINES FOR BECOMING A SMART PERSON

Guideline #5: Smart people do not automatically assume that everything they hear is true. They require substantial proof that something is true before they believe it.

Guideline #6: Smart people are not prejudiced. They do not form their opinions about something until they have carefully, with an open mind, considered *all* the information that surrounds it.

An open mind is one that is willing to believe whatever the facts reveal is true.

Guideline #7: Smart people are always re-evaluating what they think and are willing to modify their thinking if they find that it is incorrect.

Guideline #8: Smart people use their knowledge for positive rather than negative purposes.

Guideline #9: Smart people realize that their brains are crucial to intelligent thinking. Therefore, they do not do anything that would prevent their brains from functioning normally. That means smart people
- get enough sleep,
- avoid unnecessary stress, and
- do not abuse substances (such as alcohol or drugs) that can inhibit normal brain functioning.

TEN GUIDELINES FOR BECOMING A SMART PERSON

Guideline #10: Smart people constantly do things to keep their brains functioning creatively.

Smart people know that a healthy brain functions best when during every 24-hour period it receives approximately
- 8 to 10 hours of mental stimulation,
- 6 to 8 hours of distraction created by recreation such as playing and/or being entertained, and
- 8 hours of rest during sleep.

The brain is stimulated when it is required to put to use the information that it already knows.

The brain is stimulated by being exposed to information that it does *not* already know.

Printed material can be a source of new information.

Television, video, and **radio** can also be a source of new information.

Dialogue can be a source of new information.

Lectures and **demonstrations** can also be a source of new information.

Observation can be a source of new information.

Experimentation can also be a source of new information.

Most people prefer to use one or two sources of information over the others. However, no one source is better than another.

It is up to each individual to decide how he or she will gather new information.

No matter where people get their information, it is important that they **consider the source** of it.

To consider the source means to think about the context or setting in which information is given.

FOUR WAYS TO CONSIDER THE SOURCE

When smart people consider the source, they find out *who* is presenting the information and what qualifies them to do so.

Smart people disregard information from people who are not qualified to present it.

FOUR WAYS TO CONSIDER THE SOURCE

When smart people consider the source, they find out *why* the information is being presented and what the presenter hopes to accomplish.

Smart people disregard information that is presented by a person who has selfish or illogical motives for presenting the information.

FOUR WAYS TO CONSIDER THE SOURCE

When smart people consider the source, they find out the basis for the information and what proof there is that the information is valid.

Smart people disregard information that cannot be proven to be valid.

When smart people consider the source, they find out whether the information is consistent with other information that they know to be true.

Smart people disregard information that is not consistent with other information that they know to be true.

CONCLUSION

Since every person is unique and has a unique purpose in life, every person requires a unique collection of relevant information to become smart. This means that people are smart in different ways.

CONCLUSION

Smart people use relevant information to live their lives successfully. Since all people are equal, every person's collection of relevant information is important, and no one collection is more important than another. This means that no smart person can be considered smarter than another smart person. People are merely smart in different ways.

46 CONCLUSION

If you want to become a smart person, you must find out what relevant information you need to know to live your life to its fullest. Then you need to intelligently use the sources that will best help you learn the relevant information you need to know.

CONCLUSION 47

Once you have learned information that is relevant to you, you need to use it to
- survive and grow,
- accomplish necessary tasks and worthwhile goals,
- develop and maintain healthy relationships with others, and
- enjoy life.

48 CONCLUSION

Following the guidelines in this book will help you become a smart person.

www.ingramcontent.com/pod-product-compliance
Lightning Source LLC
Chambersburg PA
CBHW081408070526
44583CB00020B/2728